Welc to
Friendship

**A course that empowers
young people to discover
the need for and value of
positive friendships**

John Street

Illustrated by Simon Smith

Paul Chapman Publishing
A SAGE Publications Company
1 Oliver's Yard
55 City Road
London EC1Y 1SP

SAGE Publications Inc.
2455 Teller Road
Thousand Oaks, California 91320

SAGE Publications India Pvt Ltd
B-42, Panchsheel Enclave
Post Box 4109
New Delhi 110 017

Commissioning Editor: George Robinson
Editorial team: Wendy Ogden, Sarah Lynch, Mel maines
Illustrator: Simon Smith
Designer: Helen Weller

ISBN-10: 1-904315-30-5
ISBN-13: 978-1-904315-30-8

Printed on paper from sustainable resources
Printed in Great Britain by Cromwell Press Ltd

Dedication

This book is dedicated to my wife and children Jan, Adam, Luke, Jonah and Leah, for allowing me the time and space to work and, on occasions, take second place. You are my world.

The CD-ROM

The CD-ROM contains Acrobat PDF files as follows:

- Student Workbook COLOUR.pdf
- Student workbook BW.pdf
- Welcome Posters.pdf

You will need Acrobat Reader version 3 or higher to view and print these pages.

To print and assemble the workbook, we recommend you use high quality A4 paper (100gsm or more). Print one workbook at a time following these steps:

1. In page set-up, ensure the page is centred in the print area and that the output size is 100%.

2. Print all the odd pages of the document.

3. Reinsert the odd pages into the printer to print on the reverse.

4. Print all the even pages of the document.

5. Carefully staple along the centre line using a long-arm stapler and fold along this line.

The posters are set up to print to A4 but you can enlarge them to A3 by increasing the output percentage at the point of printing using the page set-up settings for your printer. To print at an even greater size you may wish to take the document to your local high-street printer.

Detailed instructions for photocopying and assembling the Student workbook are given on page 100.

A note on the use of gender

Rather than repeat throughout the book the modern but cumbersome 's/he', we have decided to use both genders equally throughout the range of activities. In no way are we suggesting a stereotype for either gender in any activity. We believe that you can adapt if the example you are given does not correspond to the gender of the child in front of you!

Contents

Introduction

Friendship

I'm sure everybody would agree that we are social beings and therefore in constant need of relationships with other people. We try to develop our relationships with acquaintances and colleagues into friendships and sometimes we are successful, sometimes we are not. But how many of us are still in close contact with our childhood friends? In our deepest hour of need who is there for us? Where are our countless number of 'best' friends when we need them? It is through my own experiences of losing contact with so many people that I have now realised how much easier life would be if those who really cared about me and supported me were there throughout my life. A friend is for life, not just for Christmas, and that is what this course is all about. It is designed to help young people understand the importance of friendship as a crucial part of life, but starting first with self-examination of themselves and an understanding of how we all need to develop in relationships.

Who is this course designed to help?

Teachers

This course was originally developed for working with Year 9 pupils in a school classroom but it was actually taught to Year 7 pupils and, although some of the material needed to be revised, they coped remarkably well. This course is designed for adaptation and using suitable visual aids (appropriate videos) and simplification of the terminology you could use this with Key Stage 2, 3 and 4, although it is suggested that it works best with 9 to 14 year olds.

Youth workers

This course challenges many issues around self-esteem, choices, society, family and teamwork, which are all a vital part of any youth curriculum. If you are involved in challenging and educating young people through informal settings this course can be used as a resource for related topics or, if appropriate, followed as a ten week course.

Faith groups

Although there is no use of religious terminology or input into this course there are very serious implications upon how we live our lives. If you run a youth group that involves a focus upon faith then there are plenty of opportunities for you to incorporate your teachings into the course material.

What are the benefits?

- Many young people have said that they know all about friendship and when completing the material they have indeed shown great wisdom in their responses. However, this is not just about teaching them something new but allowing them to begin the process of thinking through the issues, the problems and the benefits of supportive friendships. Some young people will say, 'I've never thought about that before,' and this is the primary aim of the course, to be a starting point in the process of relational change.

- As the course is worked through in 'friendship groups' the theory can be worked through in the classroom enabling them to support each other when the challenges arise.

- The groups are challenged as to the importance of respect, support, encouragement and positive praise towards their peers and themselves (especially in the 'Compliment Competition'). Once understood and put into practice these challenges and changes can have a positive influence upon the atmosphere and environment of their setting, especially if the whole school or club adopts this approach. It will soon be the groups who challenge negative behaviour and comments outside the classroom!

How to use this book

- This book should be used alongside the student workbook (photocopiable pages are included in the appendix). It is preferable that all the students have their own book as they will be writing their own views and ideas and sometimes personal answers to the questions that they are asked to think about. When you compare this book to the student workbook you will see the same sections but with a different layout.

- It is suggested that each session is started with an icebreaker as they can be very effective. There are various ideas after this introduction for you to use. Occasionally the icebreakers can be used at the end of the session as a reward for hard work. It is always your choice to use or lose the icebreaker except for the 'Compliment Competition' in Session 6, which is described on page 53 – this is a must (and very interesting to watch too).

- A good time to recap on the last session is after the icebreaker to remind the students what they have done. It is best to keep referring to the aims of the course, especially when taught in school, as this is not one of the usual curriculum subjects that the students are expected to study.

- Preparing well for each session will hopefully give you a good understanding of the aims of the activities.

- When introducing the aims it was found that the students became more receptive when personal illustrations were used. This was incorporated throughout the course and found to be of particular relevance at the start of each lesson. This is obviously your choice and careful consideration is needed about what you share from your personal experiences.

- After the main part of the session has been worked through allow time at the end for a reminder or informal evaluation of what has just been taught and discussed. This can be a very important time of reflection as it helps the group to consider what they have learnt as they leave the classroom.

Icebreakers

Below there is a selection of short activities intended to help the students to relax and be at ease with one another. There are many resource books available that have a wider variety of icebreakers and you can use any activities that you feel are appropriate to your group.

The Ball and Name game
Aim – to learn people's names.

Equipment needed: two tennis balls.

Form the group into a circle. Tell the group that this is a game to help them remember each other's name. It is not about who can catch and who can't. The first person throws a ball to another person in the circle. When that person catches the ball they shout out their own name and then throw the ball to another person. Keep going until the ball returns back to the first person. Everyone needs to remember the name of the person who threw the ball to them and the name of the person they throw the ball to. Do it again in the same order but this time the thrower calls out the person's name who they are throwing the ball to, and time how long it takes for the group to get the ball back to the first person. See if they can keep beating their previous time.

Variations of the game include throwing the ball in reverse and then throwing two balls at the same time – one forward and one in reverse.

Zig and Zag
Aim – to learn people's names.

Equipment needed: none.

Form the group into a circle. Tell the group that this is a game to help them remember each other's name. For this game everyone needs to know that their left becomes 'Zig' and their right becomes 'Zag'. They will also need to make sure that they are aware of the names of the people on each side of them. One person stands in the middle of the group and then walks up to any member of the group. They then say either 'Zig' or 'Zag' and count to ten very fast. By the time they reach ten the person in front of them should say the name of the person on either their left or right (that is 'Zig' would be the name of the person on their left and 'Zag' would be the name of the person on their right). If the person doesn't say the name in time they swap places and go into the middle. The previous person in the middle takes their place and needs to know the names of the people next to them. To make things more interesting later on in the game reduce the time to seven seconds and have two or three people in the middle.

Fruit Salad

Aim – to mix the group up.

Equipment needed: one chair per person.

Have each person sit on a chair in a circle. Choose three fruits, such as apples, kiwis and oranges, and name each child with a different fruit – so each fruit is represented by one third of the children. Ask for a volunteer and have that person stand in the middle of the group, then remove their chair from the circle. The person in the middle should call out one of the three fruits and all those named with that fruit should stand up and sit in another seat that is empty. Meanwhile the person who was in the middle should try and sit on a seat as well. If done correctly there should be a new person standing in the middle of the group. The person standing in the middle can also say 'fruit salad' and when this is said everybody should change places. The game stops when you have had enough!

Silent Movement

Aim – to work together without speaking.

Equipment needed: none.

Have the group stand in a circle. Choose a point in the circle and label it 'start'. Tell the group that they have to get themselves in order of birthdays, from left to right, without talking. The person with the earliest birthday will get to the 'start' point and the rest will follow around. Each person can only move one place at a time and they must therefore find out whether the person standing next to them has a birthday before or after theirs. If it is after they are to move places until they have found somebody whose birthday is before theirs and they then stand still. They can be as creative as they wish to find out the dates as long as they don't talk. At the end of the activity go round and ask them to say their birthday to see if they succeeded.

Remember?

Aim – to test the groups' power of observation

Equipment needed: a tray, a tea towel and 25 small items such as a pen, a paperclip, a sweet, a feather, a leaf, a badge, a key, a coin, pens and paper.

Put the items on the tray and place the tea towel or cloth over the items so that they cannot be seen. Give each young person a piece of paper and a pen or pencil. Place the tray in the middle of the group and tell them they have 30 seconds to look at the tray. Remove the tea towel and after 30 seconds cover the tray. The group now has two minutes to write down as many items as possible that they remember. The winner is the one who has the most number of items on their list.

Line-up
Aim – to work together as a team under pressure.

Equipment needed: none.

Clear a space and have all the group stand up on one side of the space. When you say, 'Go' they are to line up as fast as possible, in order of the subject you give them. For example, as in 'Silent Movement' (on page 10), tell them to line up in order of birthdays, only this time they can talk. Use a variety of different subjects such as house numbers, alphabetical first and last names, parents'/carers' birthdays, favourite colour, time they wake up or alphabetical pets names. Time each line-up and see if they can do it quicker next time.

Animal Pairs
Aim – to find a partner.

Equipment needed: piece of paper and a pen.

Write the names of animals on small pieces of paper, making sure that you have a piece of paper for everyone in the group. There should be at least two of the same animal on the papers (one name per piece of paper). Mix the papers up and give one to everybody in the room. The aim of the game is that each person should find their pair by making the noise of the animal on their card.

I Sit On a Hill

Aim – to mix the group up.

Equipment needed: one chair per person.

Have everyone sit on a chair in a circle with one empty chair. The person to the right of the empty chair moves places into the empty chair whilst saying 'I sit', the person on their right does the same but says 'on a hill' and the next person does the same but says 'with my friend…' They have to say the name of another person in the circle and then that person moves into the empty chair next to them. At this point the people on the left and right of the new empty chair (the one where the 'friend' was just sitting) race to sit in the empty space. The quickest one sits in the chair and says 'I sit', and so on. This keeps on going until the group is mixed up well and you are ready to move on.

Session 1

Friendship – The Beginning

Session aims

- To introduce the concept of the value of friendships, to understand why this course is as important, if not more so, as any other subject that they may learn about.

- To create an environment whereby more can be learnt about each other and everybody can feel more comfortable being around one another.

- To attempt to break down some of the barriers of emotions, such as embarrassment, feeling uncomfortable, fear and isolation.

Session background

This is the beginning not just of a new course but of the understanding and improvement of groups' relationships with their friends or potential friends. In a room full of people there will always be the confident people who can talk to anyone about anything and ones who sit in silence longing for somebody to approach them and ask the first question. Both of these people and all those in between, follow the basic principles of relationship building–they want to be accepted and feel comfortable around the other people in the room, but they first have to overcome their fears and inhibitions and believe in themselves. Even the most confident person will wonder if they've been accepted.

Our starting point in this session is to make the class aware of how everyone else in the room is feeling. At this early stage it is not about choosing who will be their lifelong friends but about recognising and overcoming the barriers that stop us from taking the first steps in relationship building. We are beginning to consider the concept that everyone in the room has the potential to be our friend.

Friendship is fickle and fragile and it can be easily broken, especially amongst groups. We are therefore looking at how to build deep foundations on solid ground that will withstand stormy and conflicting times. When we can understand how friendships work we can value them and work hard to make them strong.

Icebreaker (optional)

'The Ball and Name game' described on page 9.

Session introduction

Many young people will find it difficult to understand why they are being taught about friendship. Start the first lesson with either a video, song, poem or the following statement which is about friends and see if they can guess what the session is about.

Guess what it is?

When I'm happy I like to share it; when I'm sad I really need it; when I argue it can break; this is something hard to fake; it could last a lifetime or just a day, it takes hard work to achieve it, not money to pay. I can

14

have many of these at a time, but the special ones I'll treasure as mine. What is it?

Suggestions (see resource list in the appendix for further details):

Theme from Friends (song by The Rembrandts)
Veggie Tales – who is my neighbour? (video)
Stand By Me (film).

The introduction in the student booklet is a statement that challenges the group about the amount of effort that they put into the work and for them to see the importance of what they are studying. You will probably need to keep referring back to this aim throughout the course.

> # Introduction
>
> This course is aimed at showing you the truth and reality of friendships and whether we should value them and work at them.

Breaking down the barriers

The first few activities after the introduction are games that force the group into approaching the other people in the room and asking them questions. This will inevitably cause some feelings of embarrassment and fear, which are some of the barriers to the beginning of a new relationship. The aim of these exercises is to involve the whole group in a fun activity that takes the focus off individuals and puts it on a challenge to be completed.

Before you begin to explain the rules of each game, try and help the whole group to understand how some people might be feeling and that it's OK to have these emotions as long as they work together to overcome them. However, don't put too much focus on this and remind them that it should be fun.

embarrassment

fear

isolation

These are feelings that we don't like to experience when we're with other people. We need to try and overcome them.

Activity 1

This game is specifically aimed at getting the group to do things they would not normally do, therefore some will feel slightly embarrassed when asked. It also helps them to talk to people in the group who they may not have spoken to before. They will become consumed with the signatures so to some degree the focus is taken off their embarrassment.

Explain the rules as follows:

The rules are simple. Question one asks you to walk up to somebody in the group and ask if you can untie their shoe. If they say 'yes' you untie their shoelace and then ask them to sign your paper on the line below question one. If they want to they can ask you to complete one of their questions as well (remember – if you say 'no' so could they!). An important rule is that each person can only sign the same sheet twice. The first to gather all nine signatures is the winner.

Note: It is important for you to look out for those who are not getting involved and volunteer to do some of the tasks for them.

Activity 2

If you have time, the following game is the next stage in talking to people you are unfamiliar with. It forces the group to ask somebody else questions such as their likes and dislikes, about their family or what they've done over the weekend. The aim of the game is simply to get the other person to answer 'yes' or 'no' and through answering these questions very important and valuable information is exchanged between two people who might never have spoken to each other before.

The Sweet Game

Give each young person seven sweets (wrapped ones are better!). They have to go around the group asking people questions. If the person answering says either 'yes' or 'no' or nods their head, they have to give the other person one of their sweets.

The winner is the person with the most sweets at the end of the given time.

Discussion

At the end of the games have a discussion with the group about whether people felt uncomfortable or embarrassed and whether they enjoyed the games or not. Try and allow opportunities for the quieter people to share their thoughts and feelings with the group.

We all need friends

The next two poems will help to focus on the early stages and the frailty of friendship. Ask somebody to read them out one at a time and after each poem have a discussion about why we want friends. The poems challenge two primary issues, the first is that we choose friends because of what we can get from them and the second issue is that our friendships can change very quickly until they are established and have a strong foundation.

Tracy Venables
by Colin McNaughton

Tracy Venables thinks she's great,
Swinging on her garden gate.
She's the girl I love to hate -
'Show-off' Tracy Venables.

She's so fat she makes me sick,
Eating ice-cream, lick, lick, lick.
I know where I'd like to kick
'Stink-pot' Tracy Venables.

Now she's shouting 'cross the street,
What's she want, the dirty cheat?
Would I like some? Oh, how sweet
Of my friend Tracy Venables.

Poem from the book *There's an Awful Lot of Wierdos in our Neighbourhood* by Colin McNaughton.
© 1987 Colin McNaughton.
Reproduced by permission of Walker Books Ltd,
London SE11 5HJ

Best Friends
by Adrian Henri

It's Susan I talk to not Tracy,
Before that I sat next to Jane;
I used to be best friends with Lynda
But these days I think she's a pain.

I used to go skating with Catherine,
Before that I went there with Ruth;
And Kate's so much better at trampoline:
She's a show off, to tell you the truth.

Natasha's all right in small doses,
I meet Mandy sometimes in town;
I'm jealous of Annabel's pony
And I don't like Nicola's frown.

I think that I'm going off Susan,
she borrowed my comb yesterday;
I think I might sit next to Tracy,
She's my nearly best friend: she's OK.

Reproduced by kind permission of the Adrian Henri estate.

Bringing it all together

Sometimes we find it difficult to like somebody because of their appearance, their behaviour or because we are not sure how they will take us. Whether we know it or not we are all trying to make friends, because we are all social beings in need of friendship. We might know how lonely it can be when we have nobody to talk to or share stuff with – so we try to make friends with somebody and others try to make friends with us. We usually decide if we are going to like somebody by appearance but we should see all people as potential friends. For example, would you make friends with a rough sleeper because she looked dirty and dishevelled, even if they have a great personality?

Tell the students that we all need friends but friendship can be very fragile in its early stages. When children have an argument they generally say 'I'm not your friend anymore' and then five minutes later they're playing as if nothing has happened. As we get older it becomes harder to 'mend' what is broken. Friendship is a serious business and it takes a lot of hard work to make a friendship last, but it is well worth it to make life better and easier.

Ask the students to think about your current friendships and why you are friends with these people. Then consider the strengths and weaknesses of your friendships and whether you think they will last after you've left school.

Session 2

Life – The Reality

Session aims

- To show the group that life is actually very hard and that there is pressure from every direction trying to tell us how to live.

- To show how people's ideas and perceptions of how they should live can have a serious impact on their future lifestyle.

- To introduce the group to the choices and decisions that they have to make.

Session background

There are many things in life that we have to cope with and one of the hardest challenges for groups is coping with the difficulties of living up to other people's expectations. If we were all accepted as unique, individuals with different tastes, desires and abilities, dealing with life would be much easier. However, we are all expected to live in the mould and trend that popular culture sets, such as what clothes to wear and what music to listen to. When we choose to be different and not conform to a particular lifestyle we are regarded as strange, abnormal, weird or extreme.

Many groups are searching for their own identity and therefore choose, often sub-consciously, to belong to various sub-cultures that are classified as 'youth culture'. These are generally set by marketing strategies or extreme music, sport and cult films or television.

We all try so hard to fit into other people's expectations so that we will be accepted and liked. Sometimes the standards of those we seek to be like are out of our reach or are achievable at a great cost to us. How can we be accepted for being ourselves, allowed to choose what we want without fear of rejection or ridicule? If we cannot ask ourselves this question and answer it with conviction can we really help our group?

Icebreaker (optional)

'Zig and Zag' described on page 9

Previous session recap

This can be done as a whole-group discussion allowing the group to reflect on what they have learnt and whether they have had any experiences, since the last sessions, where they recognised any lessons learnt from the last session.

"Last session we began to consider whether all people have the potential to be our friend and we also played some games that helped us to think about our feelings when we spend time with people who we do not know very well. We looked at friends and how they can so easily change if we have friends for the wrong reasons, for example, they have things that we do not. Friendship is not about what we can get but what we can give."

Session introduction

What does perception mean? It means how you view or see something and what you expect it to be like. Some people expect that a chocolate milkshake is going to taste like chocolate and they will enjoy it very much, while somebody else might expect it to taste disgusting because they have never tried it before. They have different perceptions about the taste of chocolate milkshake.

Everyone has a different perception and expectation as to how we should live our lives. For example, some people would perceive a religious leader as perfect and are greatly shocked when they hear stories of failure and immoral behaviour. Others perceive fame and money to be the route to happiness but the rich and famous generally disagree. The British Government may think that all those between the ages of 5 and 16 should be at school and you may not agree.

We will now consider different perceptions, viewpoints or under-standings for a variety of areas of life. The aim of this activity is to try to understand why some people think that you should live your life their way and whether or not you think they are right.

Some people may convince us that their ideal or perception is right and it could have a negative influence on us. Others may have a positive impact on our lives. The question is how to recognise the difference and how to choose?

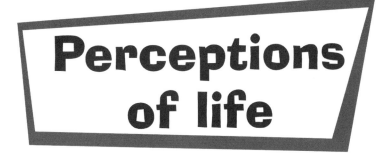

Perceptions of life

Under the influence!

Activity 1

We now move to thinking about the perception of society with a focus on popular culture and the trends that media and marketing strategies influence. Society tries to convince people that they are only 'cool' if they wear branded clothes or if they listen to a specific type of music or watch a certain programme. Popular culture is dictated by marketers trying to sell their client's latest product. If people have enough money they can keep up with changing trends but if they cannot afford to constantly change their lifestyles and possessions they will soon be classed as social outcasts. This is a huge strain for young people whose families cannot afford the latest popular items. Young people will be verbally taunted if they do not 'fit' within the cultural norms. Society's perception of life is perfection. It is unfortunate that we cannot show young people that those who market perfection are far from it themselves.

Society

We need to use this activity to help teach the group how to recognise the positive and negative influences of society and how to cope with the consequences of their choices. For example, society suggests that all girls need to be thin and blonde and boys need a six-pack stomach (negative influence), whereas other sections of society provide a diverse variety of trends complete with clothing styles, helping each person to discover their own identity and feel a level of acceptance with others who wear the same styles (positive influence).

Ask the group to discuss what they think are other perceptions of society for how we should live our lives and get them to write their answers in the space provided. You might like them to use a variety of magazines to build an image of society's perception of how we should look and live.

Activity 2

Many parents/carers would admit to wanting their children to be able to do the things that they never had the chance to do. For example, there are many young people who are expected to be the first one in their family to get a degree. There are also many families who struggle to cope with a child who has been the first in their family to be excluded from school. Families and guardians place a great deal of expectation on their children to achieve success and to be well behaved. There are also those adults who expect their children to grow up too quickly and become adults before their time. A child could be caught up in circumstances where they need to be a carer or they need to take more responsibility at home due to illness.

Whatever a young person's circumstances he should be able to consider whether his family's perceptions of his life direction is positive or negative. (For example, the family perception that homework should be completed is good as it benefits their education and career prospects are improved whereas the family perception that a person must gain a degree increases pressure to achieve what might be unachievable.)

Activity 3

One of the biggest influences on a young person is their peer group, especially for somebody who has to conform to the group in order to be accepted. Young people can sometimes be forced to make choices that go against their personal, or family's, beliefs and values in order to be accepted by their peers. For example, Shona's family may have taught her not to swear or smoke and yet in order for her to be accepted by her peer group she has to swear or smoke. Alternatively, Amrit's family norm might involve criminal activity but his friendship group might be totally opposed to crime.

Friends

Again, ask the group to discuss positive and negative influences from friendship groups and what they expect from their friends. Also ask them to discuss how they would react if a friend, or member of their friendship group, asked them to do something that they thought was wrong.

Activity 4

We end this exercise by introducing the group to the concept of self-evaluation. This is the first time that we ask the group to take a look at themselves and this will continue throughout the rest of the course. For this exercise we want them to examine their perceptions of themselves. They will need to start with something easy, but that is positive, for example do they view themselves as clever, funny, sporty, arty or good at drama? Then they can think about how they see themselves physically and then move onto more in-depth thinking about how their behaviour is influenced by those around them. For example, do they play truant because their friend does or do they call somebody else names because they think it will make their friends laugh and like them more? They can write their answers in the space provided.

Me

Once they have had time to think about themselves in this context you will find it helpful to recap this section by focusing on the impact of positive and negative influences on their lives. For example, you could say:

Activity summary

"Sometimes we choose to do things because we think other people will like us more, although we have made the wrong choice. Sometimes people want us to do things that we do not feel comfortable with or that we know are wrong. We can choose to say 'no' but we know they will make fun of us and maybe even stop being our friends. Sometimes it is very hard to know if we are being lead in a positive or negative direction and we need to learn how to make the right choices. The best way to find out which direction to take is to talk to your family and friends about why they are trying to influence you in certain ways. For example, "Why do you want me to make fun of that new boy? Is it because you want me to make you laugh because if it is I'll tell you a joke rather than making fun of somebody else."

The next step is for the group to consider the different directions that their lives can take depending upon how much they allow other people to influence their choices. The aim of this section is to compare different lifestyles and try to understand what choices people have had to make in order to reach this stage in their lives. A good way of achieving this is to compare two extreme lifestyles. (Examples are provided in the Discussion section.)

> Life is hard enough to cope with without other people telling us how we should live, what we should look like and what choices we should make to be accepted.
>
> However, the reality of life is that we need help. We are the only ones who can decide the direction we take – other people can only give us help, options and opportunities.
>
> But – we have to consider, very wisely, the choices we make. Some will be good, some will be bad.

Discussion

If you have access to a video player you could use videos that portray extreme lifestyles. These video clips will vary depending on the age and setting of your group, but examples are *Lord of the Rings* (which shows a fantasy lifestyle) and *Trainspotting* (which portrays a life of drugs and despair). For younger ages you could use *Peter Pan* and *Oliver Twist* (video details in the resources section). Other ideas for this activity could be to choose contrasting pictures from magazines or the Internet.

Select a range of images of people with attractive lifestyles and pictures of people in difficult, dangerous or unfortunate situations. After viewing alternative lifestyles ask the group what they considered to be the differences between the two extremes. Remember you are trying to direct their thoughts towards possible choices that have led these people to where they are now, for example, a person is influenced to take drugs, commits a crime in order to feed their addiction and ends up in prison, or, a person is influenced and encouraged to live their dream of acting so attends a stage school, which gives them opportunities to start an acting career and become famous.

Now you can move on to considering examples that would be closer to reality for your group. You could use a scene from *Four Weddings and a Funeral* and a scene from *The Full Monty*, *East is East* or *Billy Elliot*. All of these films show life in Britain, the first one is a realisation that money can't buy you happiness and a desperate hope to find love, and the others show how people try to make life work through struggles and hard times. If you do not have access to a video you could describe a scene from a popular television soap or read a story from a local newspaper that describes the difficulties a family or person is having. All of these images will help the group to think about their futures and consider how the choices they make now influence the direction of their lives.

Activity summary

Next you should draw the group's attention to these comments about our choices (page 8 in the student handbook). You can ask somebody to read out the comments and ask the group what they think it means or you could read out the following paragraph (or adapt it to suit your group).

"It is time for you to think about your choices. Many of you will make your choices based on the way other people want you to live. They may want you to be like them or think they know what is best for you. Some of these influences might be positive and help you to grow and develop, but sometimes you may feel pressurised or forced into making a choice that you do not want to make. Each of us has the right to ask questions about why other people want us to make a specific choice.

What you need to consider is whether the choices you make, or are forced to make, will have a positive or negative impact on the direction that you want your life to go in."

The friends we choose can be good or bad depending on whether they help us grow and support us, or whether they hold us back because they want to make us into something that we don't want to be.

Optional activity

This next section is optional and can be used if there is time. It follows on from the last paragraph which is aimed at getting the group to think about the influences that other people have on their lives. This section takes that a step further and focuses on their friends' influences.

Ask the group to read out the following paragraph:

"How much influence do your friends have on the decisions that you make? Do your friends ask you to do things, to make choices that have a negative influence on our lives, such as being rude to a teacher, stealing from a shop, playing truant, smoking or drugs? Or do your friends encourage you to make positive choices, for example, befriending a new student, not to bully, to show respect, to explore your gifts and talents?"

Response can be via an open discussion, or by quietly contemplating answers and writing them down in their books. Alternatively they can discuss this with their friends (if they are sitting near them) and consider their friends' responses.

Bringing it all together

To summarise the session you should read out the following statements (also in the handbook on page 8):

The future is not only a place you are travelling to but a life you are creating.

"Every choice you make has an effect on the direction of your life. If you commit a crime you could end up in prison and not fulfil your childhood dreams. If you know what you want to do in the future you need to consider the choices you make now and how other people try and influence you. The choice is yours!"

Session 3

Life – The Journey

Session aims

- To help the group to think about life as a journey that we all travel on. On this journey there are things that we can control and things that we can't and some of the choices we make will change our lives forever.

- To introduce the group to the realm of positives and negatives, good and bad, particularly in the context of choices that determine the direction and events of our lives.

Session background

This session is based on a belief that, in general, our lives are full of ups and downs, pain and happiness, failure and success. Not many people will reach the end of their lives, look back and say, "I have lived a good and easy life."

I believe that life is hard, and for some it's pure survival. However there are those who appear to have an easy life with too much materialism and good living, but they still suffer from boredom and dissatisfaction. It doesn't seem to matter what your personal circumstances or living environment, whether you were born into wealth or poverty, whether you have a difficult family background or belong to a large loving family – life is not easy to cope with on your own!

We are social beings with a deep desire and need to be with and accepted by other people. Even isolated monks who have chosen to be cut off from civilisation live in a community. We all need to be with or near other people and when these people are not available, supportive or understanding we find that life becomes that little bit harder to deal with.

Life's difficulties are made easier when we have people around us who become deeply involved with our lives.

The journey of life is a very difficult road to travel, especially if we are lonely and isolated. Life is not easy at all and this session will hopefully encourage the group to consider who they are travelling with and how these people are influencing the shape and direction of their lives.

Icebreaker (optional)

'Fruit Salad' described on page 10.

Previous session recap

Last session we looked at perceptions and viewpoints. Then we went on to consider different lifestyles and how the choices we make can sometimes have a big effect on where we will end up in the future. We also touched upon the way that the people around us influence our decisions and the choices that we make.

Session introduction

Is life easy?

Introducing this session, in a whole-group context, with the question, "Is life easy?" will give a good foundation to the rest of the session. The young people you have in your group may think they have a good understanding of life and how to handle difficulties and conflicts. They may say that life is about what you can get out of it and the way to solve problems is to use violence and aggression. This may indeed be the culture or environment that they currently live in. When asked the question, "Is life easy?" they may think they know all about life, and this will be reflected through their answers. In response to their answers ask them how they would cope if an earthquake hit their street and their home was demolished. An extreme scenario maybe but it will begin to help them to realise that life has many unexpected difficulties. At some point in the opening discussion you, as the facilitator, could share some personal examples of your own experiences of life's hardships. Bearing in mind the amount of personal information that should be revealed to the group you could mention any family illnesses, bereavements or choices that you have made that have changed your life (such as taken the wrong job or relationships). You should remember that this is an introduction to the lesson and the next exercise will involve the young people thinking about their own responses to different areas of life, so try not to spend an excessive amount of time on this question.

Me and my world

Activity 1

This exercise focuses on five areas of our lives, the world, our country, our community, our family and ourselves. As the group think about these different areas they will be thinking about the things in life that are considered good and the things that are considered bad. Each person may have different perceptions of what is good and bad and this will be reflected in their discussions and answers. It will be useful if the young people complete this exercise in small groups, and change groups after each section so that they share ideas with other people in their group. They may prefer to do the last section on their own unless they want some suggestions from their friends.

For each of the five sections they will need to discuss, in their groups, what they consider to be the good things and the bad things for each heading. Ask them to write some of their answers in the spaces provided in their handbooks.

Examples are:

	Good	**Bad**
Global	nature, animals	war, famine
National	football	unemployment
Community	play areas	crime
Family	get-togethers	arguments
Me	good at maths	temper tantrums

These are only possible examples and many different answers will be discussed.

Activity summary
The feedback time can be carried out either at the end of the whole exercise or after each section has been completed. Write their answers on the board or flip-chart under the appropriate headings. You may want to allow extra time for discussions related to any important issues that have been raised.

Discussion

With the list of answers that you have just written ask the group to make a choice as to which ones they think they have control over and which ones they cannot control. For example, we cannot control whether it is going to rain today but we can control our tempers.

34

Next ask the group why they think that they cannot control things like crime in their community or war then explain that in general terms we do not have any control over the actions or thoughts of other people, although we may be able to influence them. The only thing we have true control over is ourselves.

What do we really need to make it through life?

Life is a journey.

Some things we can control, some things we can't.

What do we really need to make it through life?

Activity 2

As the facilitator you need to help the group grasp an understanding of their ability to control themselves, their actions, words and thoughts. A good example of this is found in the film *Forest Gump* (details in the Resource section). It shows two stages of Forest's life, one during his early years and the next towards the end of his teenage life. There is a group of boys who throw stones at him on both occasions. The film clips represent the journey of a boy through several years where he cannot and does not control the actions of other boys. He is also unable to influence their choice to bully him and the only advice his one friend can offer is to run! If you do not have access to a video player then you can read or describe a story that has a similar focus of people choosing to bully somebody else and the bullied person not having control, for example, Cinderella. If there is time you could ask the group to create a drama or mime showing this scenario.

You can then say to the group as a whole, "This session has been about control, but not how we can control other people, but how we can learn to control ourselves. Our actions, thoughts and attitudes towards others can be negative and it is only us who can change them. We need to learn how to challenge ourselves and make the necessary changes."

You may want to return to the previous exercise and focus on the 'me' box to see if anything that they have written can be challenged and changed about themselves following the previous discussions.

Bringing it all together

The session's final thoughts consider the question in the student book, "what do we really need to make it through life?" The obvious answers will be food, clothes, water and oxygen and possibly somebody might say 'love' or 'family'. End the session by saying, "If we think that the answer is other people we need to learn how to relate towards other people. There may be times when our attitudes or behaviour are negative and we upset people. If we did this with everyone we would not have any friends and would starve ourselves of our basic needs for companionship. You can make the choice to be nice and caring or to be cruel and nasty. How are you going to control yourself and what choices are you going to make?"

Session 4

The Making of a Friend

Session aims

- To help the group to think about the differences between people they do not like and do not want to be with and those whom they think are fantastic and long to be like.

- To think about the characteristics and 'make-up' of an ideal friend.

Session background

We are beginning to guide the group's thoughts towards the qualities needed for good, strong, long lasting friendships. The group may have never critically analysed the qualities that their friends, or potential friends, have and they are more likely to have a simplistic thought process following the line 'If I like somebody they can be my friend'. I believe that there are many people who want to become friends with the rich, the successful, the strongest and the beautiful, and this is the same for both young people and adults. This, I believe, is due to man's inherent need for acceptance and the belief that this is best achieved with the 'perfect' people of this world. It may be a useful exercise for you, as the facilitator, to consider your own process of choosing friendships and how you have responded to the 'perfect' people you have met.

This session begins to explore the reasons behind our choices. We will be looking at questions like, "What is it that makes us want to be with certain people?", "What is it about them that we idolise and try to imitate?" and "Why do we refuse to get close to some people and reject them simply by their appearance?" We have already considered the effects that society has on us and its perception of perfection. I am suggesting here that we all want to be liked, to be accepted and all too often it means that we go out of our way to 'fit in' with a certain group, particularly the 'in crowd'.

When we can analyse and understand why we feel embarrassed by or near some people and what attracts us to others, we can begin to recognise why we reject some people and why we try desperately to be accepted by others.

Icebreaker (optional)

'Silent Movement' described on page 10.

Previous session recap

"In the last session we looked at whether life is easy to get through or whether there are going to be difficult times and problems for us to face. We considered how many things we can control and what will happen that we cannot stop, like earthquakes and exams and whether we call somebody a name or tell a lie. Some things we can control and these help us to be better friends but others we choose not to control and who will be our friend then?"

Session Introduction

Introduce this session to the whole group by saying, "There are many different types of people in this world, some of them you would really like to be with (like pop stars or film stars) and some people you would be reluctant, or even anxious, to spend time with because they appear or behave in a way which is threatening (such as rowdy football fans or people who are drunk). Today we are going to start thinking about what it is that attracts us to some people and keeps us away from others."

First impressions count

Activity 1

Inform the group that you want them to use their imaginations as they are about to describe a person who they would least like to be seen with (in their words – wouldn't be seen dead with). If you have an imaginative group you can allow them to start describing this person now, alternatively you can read out the following scenario:

"You are going to the biggest party of the year, all your mates will be there; it will be the place to be. There is also a very special boy going who you really want to impress – tonight could be his lucky night. You have been planning your outfit, your moves, even what you are going to say. On your way out of the door your mum (or appropriate person), tells you that you have to take your younger brother with you. The problem is that he always seriously embarrasses you wherever you go."

Describe the most embarrassing person

Ask them to describe (write or draw) what it is about this person that would make them feel completely embarrassed and know that they will never be accepted by the special person after tonight. It could be that their brother picks his nose and flicks the snot at people or wears really un-trendy clothes. It may be more fun for the pupils to do this activity in pairs so that they can discuss their ideas and have a laugh about their thoughts and answers.

Some of the group will not have any younger brothers. Remind them that they are to be imaginative and create a fictitious person. It is not important whether they have a brother or not but what it is about a person that they would be completely embarrassed about.

They may also struggle with the concept of being imaginative or describing somebody. If so, give them examples of stereotypical people who are considered an embarrassment, such as a very drunk person in an unsuitable situation. We want them to be as descriptive as possible about the things that they really don't like and for the majority of young people this will be their physical appearance, actions and behaviour.

Activity summary

After the group have had time to describe an embarrassing person bring the group back together and have an open discussion about their thoughts and perceptions. You can write their answers on a board using two different headings – physical appearance and inner qualities. During this feedback session there may be some answers given that you feel need to be addressed there and then, for example, a young person may say that they would be really embarrassed if somebody had loads of spots on their face. You may have another young person in the room who has acne and is seriously affected by this comment. You can address this issue by saying the following, "There is a definite need for difference in this world. What do you think the world would be like if everyone was the same? We need to look at our own physical appearance and consider what is different about us compared to everyone else in the class. Then we need to think about how we would feel if people were embarrassed about our differences."

Discussion

The necessity for deeper discussion depends on whether their answers have a significant effect on another member of the group. If you feel that the conversation does not become personal to anyone in the group you can move on to the next part of this activity. We look at the issue of physical self-examination in more depth in Session 6.

Activity 2

Describe your ideal person

We now move on to the second part of this activity, which is the opposite of the first. Use the same scenario of the party scene but this time use the following to guide their imagination:

"You are going to the same party but this time you meet up with your friends. Again you are hoping to meet and impress this very special girl. There are many things about this particular person that you like. She is amazing and you dream of becoming just like her. Once you have a picture in your mind of this person write or draw a description of her in your books. You need to consider what it is about her that makes her so special. What do you like about her and why?"

Depending on the age of your group you can help them by suggesting that this person could be a famous pop star, a girl or boy that they have fancied for ages, or a local 'star'. They should be trying to describe what it is about this person that makes them worthy of attention or even envy.

Again it may be more fun for the pupils to do this activity in pairs so that they can discuss their ideas and have a laugh about their thoughts and answers.

Discussion

After the group have had time to describe their ideal person you can again bring the group back together and have an open discussion about their thoughts and perceptions. You can write their answers on a board or flip-chart using the same headings – 'physical appearance' and 'inner qualities'.

It is highly unlikely that anyone will be offended by the feedback about an ideal person, but be prepared to discuss anything that you think will upset or concern another member of the group. An example of this may be that a young person is impressed by somebody who smokes and takes drugs, or who bullies anyone who doesn't do what they say. These may well be seen by some young people as ideal and perfect, somebody they envy, and if this is the case then refer back to Session 2 where we looked at the positive and negative influences of other people on the decisions we make and the directions our lives take.

After you have finished the second feedback bring the group's attention to the descriptions of both the embarrassing and ideal people. Ask the group if they agree with all the answers or whether there are any difference of opinions. For example, there may be somebody who thinks their ideal person should be rich and for other members of the group money may not be important.

During these discussions you will be asking the group to think about feelings and attitudes, which they may not have been able to do before, so be patient and flexible allowing time for the discussions.

Bringing it all together

The aim of this discussion is to allow the group time to start thinking about the qualities and characteristics that they look for in their friends. When the discussion is coming to an end ask the group to write down their five main priorities, from the feedback lists or from their own workbooks, that they consider necessary for friendship. They can use the space provided in their workbooks at the bottom of page eleven.

Please note: this final part of the session is purely a thought provoker that brings together all that has been looked at during this session and leads the group into the next chapter which looks at the qualities of friendship in more detail.

So what makes a good friend?

Session 5

The Heart of Friendship

Session Aims

- To move away from the external qualities that attract us to some people and consider the internal characteristics, values and attitudes needed to make friendship last.

Session background

In the last session we began the process of considering the basic qualities and characteristics of friendship, but this was focused around our perceptions and ideals, our idols or the people we want to be like. The group probably began with describing a person's looks or their possessions before considering character, values and principles.

In this session we will take those initial perceptions and descriptions of friendship, given by your group in the previous lesson, and consider whether their attributes and qualities will stand under the pressure of difficult times or conflict. We begin by looking at other people's friends and their need for friendship but then we make it more personal to the group as they begin to think about their own friendships. We are moving from the external attractions of being with somebody to discovering the 'inner-beauty' of a true friend. The second part of this session presents scenarios that will question whether the group's existing friendships were formed by outward appearances, materialism or a deep desire to be accepted, or whether they have friendships with strong foundations of acceptance, support and encouragement.

The final question presented to the group is the most personal – what kind of friend are you? Friendship is a two way process and their initial self-examination becomes more challenging as they begin to look at their own involvement with the friends they have now and in the future.

Icebreaker (optional)

'Remember?' described on page 11.

Previous session recap

"Last session we looked at embarrassing people and those we most want to be like. We considered the differences between the two and tried to understand what really makes a good friend – is it the things they have or their looks? Or is it what's inside that counts?"

Session introduction

To start this session we need the group to think about personal difficulties and the need for supportive friends. You can use any of the following or come up with your own ideas:

Video – a scene from *Friends* (series 2, episode 9). This is an excellent scene as one of the characters is going to meet her dad for the first time. She therefore takes along two of her best friends for support.

Fairytale Story – The *Wizard of Oz*, how Dorothy needed her new friends to help her get home.

Current Media – You could also use a current chart song, soap episode or newspaper article if you can find one that is appropriate.

The aim of this exercise is to ask questions about the characters' friendship, such as:

● Why did they need their friends' support?

● Could they have coped on their own in this situation?

● What makes them good or bad friends?

At the end of this introduction help the group to realise that they are beginning to discover a deeper understanding of friendship, that involves commitment and support, time and energy, unconditional love and encouragement.

Activity 1

The next exercise focuses on how people respond and react to certain issues. You can ask them, "Do you know your friends well enough to be able to say how they would react to a specific problem?", "Would you always expect your friends to support you or agree with you, even if you were in the wrong?" and "Would you expect your friends to stand up for you and support you through tough challenges that you face?"

Discuss:

- How would your friends react if they saw you go into a shop and steal some sweets?
- How would your friends react if you tried to get them to do something wrong?
- How would your friends react if you got them into trouble?
- How would your friends react if you were choosing sides in a game and you didn't pick them?

This is a difficult and hard-hitting reality exercise to test the strength of any friendship.

There are more scenarios following for you to use.

The questions on the previous page are potential real life issues that young people may be affected by. Any of these issues could have a significant impact on their relationship with their friends that could either strengthen or destroy their relationship depending on the decisions that are made. Below are further scenarios for them to consider. You will need to choose which questions suit your group's age and ability and feel free to create your own scenarios that might be more appropriate:

Age 9 – 10

- How would your friends react if you stopped sharing your things with them?
- How would your friends react if you went to play with somebody who they didn't like?

Age 11 – 12

- How would your friends react if they offered you a cigarette and you said 'no'?

- How would your friends react if they saw a member of your family hitting you?

Age 13 –14

- How would your friends react if they offered you drugs and you said 'no'?

- How would your friends react if you had a car accident and became wheelchair bound?

Discussion

Allow the group time to consider the questions on their own and then give them space to discuss their answers within their friendship groups or with the person sitting next to them. If they do discuss it with their friends, and they are close friends, they should have similar answers and hopefully they will begin to understand the qualities of good friendship. This may cause conflicting opinions if, for example, one friend expects the other to take drugs and the other friend expects them to respect their decision to say 'no'. This is a good opportunity for the group to discuss their preference for boundaries in their friendships and also to consider whether their current friends fall within those boundaries!

Activity 2

During the group's discussions from the previous exercise they will have considered characteristics and attributes that are associated with true, positive friendship. These may include external attributes like being helpful, sharing, always being there, a shoulder to cry on and supportive and internal attributes such as love, kindness, understanding and challenging.

In their course books ask the group to consider these internal and external qualities and to then write them around the following picture. They can use arrows to point to the heart for words associated with our character or soul, they can make lists on either side of the person or they can decide their own preference for placing the words they have chosen.

Bringing it all together

Have your friends got what it takes? Have you?

The final challenge for the group is for them to consider all that they have done during this session and to ask themselves these questions:

- Do my friends have the qualities and attributes that I need in a friend?

- Do I have the qualities and attributes that my friends expect and do these qualities match my own ideals for friendship?

If all the previous exercises have been successful these two very challenging questions will help the group to evaluate their current friendships and discover what type of friends they really need and what type of a friend they need to become.

Session 6

A Closer Look at Me

Session aims

- To help the group to consider how they see themselves compared to how other people do and the effects that this has on them.

- To help them to think about self-acceptance regardless of their differences.

Session background

Having looked at the qualities of friendship the group might have been challenged as to their own qualities, attributes and ability to be a good friend. If a young person discovers that they are a good friend it will boost their confidence and self-esteem. If they have realised that they have weaknesses in their relationships and they already feel bad about themselves or struggle with their own identity and esteem they may have found the last session very difficult and negative, highlighting their own beliefs that they are a failure.

This session focuses on these negative thoughts and will help the group to see themselves in a positive way. There are no perfect friends in this world because there are no perfect people and to expect an idyllic friend is very naïve. We all make mistakes, especially where relationships are concerned. We are not trying to create perfection in friendship here but to uncover the misconceptions and fallacies that are associated with friendship. The group need to come to a point whereby they have accepted themselves and are able to cope with how other people view them.

If the group can learn how to accept themselves, and actually like themselves, they will be able to appreciate their outer and inner qualities regardless of how others see them. Inner strength and inner beauty are developed over time but the starting point is to realise that how we look is okay no matter what others may say.

Icebreaker (optional)

Compliment Competition described in the session introduction on the next page.

Previous session recap

There are times in our life when we go through difficulties and we would be able to cope a lot easier if we had friends who were supportive and helped us through. We considered how our friends react in the tough times and whether they have got what it takes to be a good friend and also whether we have got what it takes to be a good friend.

Session introduction

This session has the only icebreaker that you are advised to use. It is called 'Compliment Competition' and involves two people standing at the front, taking it in turns to say something nice about the other person. Why is this a competition? It's because anyone who tries this will find it difficult as it is not in most people's nature to compliment somebody else. The rules are simple – they cannot use the same compliment twice, one person cannot repeat what the other has just said, each compliment must be said within five seconds of the previous one.

Most young people will want to 'blaze' or 'diss' (disrespect) the other person and they will find it very difficult to say something nice. This game actually challenges many different issues, like:

- We do not compliment each other enough.

- If somebody compliments us we don't know how to respond – we usually think they are being sarcastic.

- Most compliments will be about external looks rather than qualities, character or abilities.

Adults find this just as difficult as children, so have a practice with a friend first!

Activity 1

This next exercise helps the pupils to see how they see themselves and how their friends see them. Using a mirror ask them to draw a picture of how they view themselves. Ask them to try to include details like their nose, ears or spots. They will generally either hide or over emphasise the parts of their face that they are unhappy with.

My view

My friend's view

Once they have finished ask them to exchange books with a friend (or somebody sitting by them). They are then to draw how they see the other person in the space provided. Each student should have two drawings of themselves in their own book, one which shows how they see themselves and another that shows how their friends see them.

The two drawings will probably be very different. Ask them, in their pairs, to discuss any differences between the drawings and then have a group discussion about how sometimes we look at ourselves and think that there are things wrong with us. We might think that other people are laughing at the size of our nose or ears when actually they don't even notice any differences.

However, there may be some people who enjoy making fun of those who are different and if this is the case a discussion could be held about how we all have differences, that is what makes us unique individuals and we should respect the differences rather than make fun of them.

The next stage of this session is built on the first two activities, the compliment competition and the mirror image. The pupils will probably have discovered how difficult it is to compliment other people, particularly when it relates to their inner qualities. They may have also identified areas of their own physical appearance that they are unhappy with and whether their friends have noticed or commented on these differences.

The Daily Dreamer

Activity 2

We are now asking the group to become even more vulnerable by allowing their session partners to write a description of them. They should each come up with a newspaper storyline where their partner is a hero who has carried out an amazing act of bravery. Ask the students to describe their partner and to be honest about the things that they see in this person. They can start with a physical description if required and then move on to the inner qualities and character that has been shown in this act of bravery. The aim of this exercise is to help each pupil to understand how their friends, or other people, see them. If this is done properly the pupils who have a low self-view will see exactly how their friends see them and should hopefully have their negative perceptions challenged, even erased. Obviously this could become quite painful for some pupils if their 'friends' are cruel towards them and they highlight the person's greatest fears, so please be aware of potential problems and how you will deal with them. If the issue of cruelty is raised you can refer back to Session 2, where we considered how other people's choices have an effect on our growth as a person.

Discussion

After they have completed this exercise the group should spend some time reading each other's articles and discussing them. After an appropriate amount of time bring the group together and ask whether any of the pupils have had their self-views challenged.

Bringing it all together

The summary of this session should focus firstly on how the group think other people see them and the effects that this has on their friendships. This is also a challenge to those young people who think that other people's differences are something to make fun of rather than something to value. The second part of the summary should focus on how they view themselves. It might be OK for them to say that they don't care what other people think about them but if they cannot learn to accept themselves 'warts and all', to accept the things they cannot change, then they will always think that other people are making fun of them and their relationships will always struggle to grow in the area of acceptance.

Young people generally want others to accept them for who they are and they will inevitably be hurt and feel rejected if their friends try to change them or tease them about their differences. If somebody has learnt to be happy and accept herself they will be emotionally more prepared to extinguish the flames of cruelty and words that inflict the pain of rejection.

> **If we want our friends to accept us the way we are, we first need to learn to accept ourselves for who we are.**

Session 7

A Unique Individual?

Session aims

- To help the group to consider, in more depth, how they view and accept/reject themselves and to hopefully help them to recognise that they are very special and unique.

- To help them to realise that when they are happy with who they are, they will be very good at accepting other people, regardless of their differences, and this will help them become a very good friend.

Session background

Building on from the ideas of self-acceptance we now direct the students thoughts towards their self-esteem and confidence. You may have some young people in your group who are naturally very confident and this will be a good opportunity for them to consider what makes them confident. They may even help the rest of the group to identify their individual strengths and weaknesses in the area of confidence.

This session is aimed at helping a person to learn how to become more confident through having a positive self-view, and to consider the barriers that we have to overcome in order to reach a certain level of confidence.

The best example that I have used to begin this session is the film *The Mask* starring Jim Carey. The catchphrase used in this film is 'from zero to hero' and the whole concept of the story is that a man who has a very negative image of himself becomes everything that he has ever dreamed of through wearing a magic mask. It may not be possible for you to use this film in your group setting but it is advised that the use of masks, in any format, is an ideal starting point with this session.

We are trying to show the students that self-acceptance and a healthy self image can help to give us the confidence to be our normal selves with other people, rather than to wear a mask and be what we think other people want us to be.

Icebreaker (optional)

'Line-up' described on page 11.

Previous session recap

Last session we looked at how we see ourselves, because sometimes we think others don't like us or laugh at us as we think they see our imperfections. But we might find that other people do not see the imperfections in our physical appearance and actually see the good things that we have to offer. This should help us to accept ourselves for who we are and not worry what other people think.

Session introduction

The aim of this first exercise is to pull together all the underlying themes of the previous six sessions. We have discussed that we are sometimes not allowed to be who we want to be because of other people's perceptions of what they think we should be like and that this causes us to try to be something that we are not just to please them and be accepted by them. If this is the case we are actually wearing masks to hide the real us and when we start to accept and like ourselves for who we really are we can begin to take off the masks that we wear and start living the way we want.

The masks we wear

Activity 1

If it is possible to access a television and video it is recommended that you use a scene from the film *The Mask* starring Jim Carey. Towards the beginning of the film the main character, Stanley, finds a mask and when he puts it on he becomes everything he wants to be but hasn't had the confidence to become before.

Other suggested ideas, if the above is unobtainable, is to let the group use images, drawings or photos of their idols, the people they would most like to be, and put the pictures on masks. You could then ask them to act as though they were that person and see how they respond.

A healthy self-image gives us confidence.

Discussion

After the first activity has finished hold a group discussion about self-image and how we see ourselves, both externally and internally. What are the positive things that we could like about ourselves and what are the negative things that we're not so keen on? Examples are, "I am good at..." or "I am loved because..." and "I have a big nose" or "I am no good at football". (You may want to use fictitious characters to begin with if the group are not ready for open vulnerability or would find it too hard not making fun of somebody's answers.)

The more things that we like about ourselves, the more confidence we will have in ourselves and how we act around others. Continue the discussion by looking at the benefits of being confident.

Activity 2

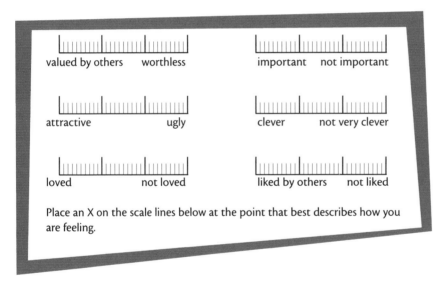

valued by others   worthless

important   not important

attractive   ugly

clever   not very clever

loved   not loved

liked by others   not liked

Place an X on the scale lines below at the point that best describes how you are feeling.

This exercise is designed to help the group to consider, at a more specific level, some of the feelings that they may have about themselves. You may need to talk them through so that the students have the same understanding of each word. For example, some people may consider themselves valued by others but when they actually think about it this may only be because they lend or give their friends material possessions. It is best if each pupil does this activity on their own so that they can be honest with themselves about how they are feeling. After this exercise you will need to affirm with the group that although this is how they might be feeling at this moment they only see it from their point of view and it might produce a false perception of their relationships and how others see them.

Activity 3

Complete this sentence:

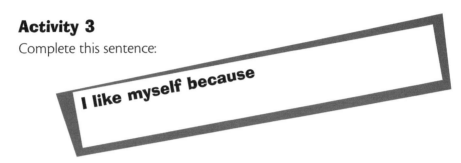

I like myself because

This next exercise is aimed at being more positive and focusing on the things that the group like about themselves. Try to ask them to fill the space with as many different things as possible, such as their personal qualities, abilities in sport, education or being great with computers. Some of them may write about other people ("I like myself because my mum helps me with my homework,") but they should try and focus on themselves rather than on other people who have an influence on them.

Activity 4

This is another exercise that allows the group to think about themselves and whether they are content with who they are or have areas they need to work on. If necessary ask the group to think of some more statements that are true and false about their own lives.

True or false?

> ▸ I never feel happy with what I have done.
> ▸ I can accept compliments from other people.
> ▸ I don't like it when people criticise me.
> ▸ I think I am below average.
> ▸ When I meet someone new, I worry if they will like me.
> ▸ I like being me.

Bringing it all together

You are a very special and unique individual. Once you can love yourself because you are you, you can become very good at accepting other people for who they are. This will make you a very, very good friend.

The summary of this session should highlight that we are all unique individuals with differences that need to be celebrated and valued, not condemned or criticised. By identifying how we feel and how others actually perceive us we can begin to deal with the barriers that prevent us from liking ourselves and feeling confident about our abilities and relationship skills.

Session 8

Do I Have a Choice?

Session aims

- To help the group to think about the choices they make and the positive and negative consequences of their decisions.

- To consider the different ways in which students act and behave at home in the family setting and with their friendship groups.

Session background

As you plan for this session you may feel that another lesson on acceptance is unnecessary, but although the first exercise continues with the theme of personal change in order to be accepted, the remainder of the session is a direct challenge on parental and peer pressure that leads to negative influences and different responses in each setting. It also challenges the way the group are accepted at home and their different patterns of behaviour between family and friends.

This session also provides an opportunity for the group to consider the impact that their families have on them and the choices they make. There are many people who have an idea of how we should live our lives and they consciously or subconsciously force their ideas on us in an effort to lead us in the direction that they think is best. This is evident with the phrase 'pushy mums' who are parents who see an ability or talent in their child's life and keep putting pressure on their child to achieve and become successful. It is also evident with friends who convince their peers to join in with criminal activity or trying drugs for the first time. Peer pressure and parental pressure is very, very strong and does not always take us in a positive direction or at least the direction that we want to go ourselves. The question we are going to ask is, 'do we have control over the choice we make and how we live our lives?' (you can also refer back to Session 2 for positive and negative influences on our choices).

Icebreaker (optional)

'Animal Pairs' described on page 11.

Previous session recap

Last session we looked at the fact that we are all unique people. We may have a variety of differences from other people and these are to be celebrated and valued rather than laughed at and scorned. We also considered our own lives and the things we like about ourselves. Having a healthy self-image will help us to accept ourselves and other people, especially those who are different.

Session introduction

Start this activity by asking the group to:

"Think about the last session and the things that you like or dislike about yourselves. Some of them you can change and some of them you have to learn to live with. During the last session the focus was on you as an individual but this time we are considering any area of life, including material possession, looks, careers, families, friends and anything else that you can think of. We are trying to see if the way you live your life is because you want to be accepted or because that's just the way it is."

Happiness is…?

Activity 1

What would make you happy?

What would you change?

Ask them the following question: "If you could change anything about your life what would you change?" As the example pictures in the workbook show it could be money, fame, physique, intellect, sporting abilities or the possessions they have. Some of the students may even go deeper than this and suggest inner changes like their temper or stopping lying.

Some people might have already decided that they are happy with themselves and do not wish to change anything. For those who do want to change something ask them to write their answers in the space provided and then hold a group discussion as to the reasons why some people still want to change, and whether this is because they are looking for acceptance.

For example, if a young person says they want to be rich and buy a fast, expensive car ask if the reason behind it is so their friends will think they are 'cool' and they will be liked more.

Once again we are helping the group to recognise who has the most powerful influences on the decisions that they make, them or somebody else?

Activity 2

This next activity is an ideal opportunity to engage in drama or to use photographic stills. The aim is for the group to think about how they respond and act when they are with their parents/carers and whether they behave differently when they are with their friends. A simple example to start with is the use of swear words. They may not swear in front of their parents/carers or other relatives because they know they would be in trouble but they may consider it normal to use swear words in everyday conversation with their peers. Hold a brief discussion as to why this is. Then get them into small groups and decide on various forms of behaviour that are different between home and with their friends and create a short dramatic sketch to highlight these. They could also use the freeze frame technique of creating a succession of photographic stills that portray the progression of a scene, if they don't want to use drama.

For example, if the issue is smoking the first freeze frame might be a group of friends together and one of them has their hand stretched out as though offering a cigarette to another person in the group. The second still could be them all smoking together and the third still could be one of them being sick because it's their first time smoking. The fourth still could be the home setting where their mum, dad or carer are smoking and the same young person is standing watching them. The fifth still could be the young person lighting a cigarette in front of their parents/carers and the final still could be the parents/carers with arms raised in shock and anger.

A very important part of the drama and freeze frames is being able to portray the different reactions that their families and friends would show, bearing in mind that families have tighter boundaries and are usually more judgmental, punishing or rebuking of behaviour, whilst friends will very often encourage, provoke and laugh at behaviour considered unacceptable at home or school.

Family   Friends

When you are with your friends do you behave differently than when you are with your family?

Discussion

How do you think your friends try to be accepted?

How do you try to be accepted?

We all want to be loved and accepted for who we are.

After an adequate time period bring the whole group together and allow each smaller group to perform their sketches. At the end of this hold a discussion about how we choose to act differently and what effects our choices have on the positive or negative direction of our lives (referring back to Session 2). The discussion should focus on how their need for acceptance by both families and friends causes them to make these different choices. If, after following the previous sessions, the group have begun to recognise their need to accept and like themselves there is a significant difference in their choices. If their friends ask them to do something they do not want to do they can refuse, knowing that their security is in themselves and not in their need to be accepted by their peers. The same can be said with families but this is harder to challenge when family members expect the children to do as they are told! Mutual respect and communication is the key to solving relational conflict (see the last session for the art of communication).

> **We all want to be loved and accepted for who we are.**

Bringing it all together

You can end the session by reading the following or using your own words:

"Sometimes our behaviour is different when we are with our family than when we are with our friends. This can cause our life's direction to be compromised if we choose to behave in ways that we know are wrong. We need to look at the big picture of our lives and see if the pressure to make the wrong choices now will affect the way that we want our lives to be in the future. It is very hard to tell somebody that we choose not to follow them, but we will sometimes need to sit down with the person and discuss the reasons why and the negative influence that we think their requests will have on us. It is a tough thing to do because it is not the normal way that we deal with issues or other people, but if you want to be in control of your life and make the right choices then you have to work at challenging the things that will stop you reaching your dreams."

Session 9

It Takes Two to Tango

Session aims

- To help the young people to understand the nature and concept of teamwork.

- To help the group to identify their strengths and weaknesses in a group setting and to build confidence in their abilities to perform as part of a team.

- To consider how effective teamwork can influence building effective relationships.

Session background

In this session we are looking at the premise that a group of people are considered a team if they are working together to achieve a common goal. It could be a sports team trying to win a championship, a team of aid workers trying to stop an outbreak of disease or a group of friends who want to support each other through adolescence.

This team can only be effective if they recognise each other's abilities and support their weaknesses and encourage them in their strengths. A successful team will consist of individuals who put the other members of their team first and recognise that they need each other to reach the goal or achieve their success.

Depending on the different friendship groups that you have within your group this could become a very difficult session if the focus is on finishing the task and competing against the other groups. The lessons that we want the group to learn are through the evaluation of how each team member has performed. As the facilitator you may also find it very frustrating to watch the groups and your natural reaction will be to offer guidance. The group will learn more from your observational comments afterwards rather than from your involvement in the task, so please allow them to get on with it, even if they do not finish the task.

Icebreaker (optional)

'I Sit On a Hill' described on page 12.

Previous session recap

Last session we asked ourselves how much control we have over the choices in our lives and whether we would change anything to make us happier. We also considered whether we behave differently with our family than with our friends and whether this is because of our need to be accepted. Who has the most influence over the choices we make, friends, family or ourselves?

Session introduction

Each person needs to see himself or herself and accept each other as a valuable member of the team. You could even start with an icebreaker that shows this, like giving everyone a jigsaw piece and telling them that they have to make the jigsaw by putting their own piece in the puzzle – nobody else can do it for them. A short discussion could follow about how each jigsaw piece is needed and should be valued in order to complete the picture and how this is similar to the roles we take on in effective teamwork.

Together we can do it

Activity 1

Allow the pupils to get into groups of four. This may be a challenge in itself so if there are any difficulties with people being left out, gently remind them that they have been looking at friendship for the past eight sessions and that this involves supporting everyone, whoever they are!

You are going to attempt a challenge.

They are going to attempt a challenge but before they begin they have to decide which role each of them is going to play. The roles they have to choose from are as follows:

- A – **leader** (somebody who focuses on the whole group, organises them, makes the final decisions, encourages all members to join in, supports, unites the group and keeps time).

- B – **designer** (somebody who focuses on the aim, gathering ideas from the group, using creativity, originality and questions any practicalities of the task).

- C – **worker** (somebody who is a 'behind the scenes' type of person and just gets on with the job, or just does what they are asked without any fuss or shows great initiative).

- D – **evaluator** (somebody who focuses on how the group functions as a team and will describe how each person reacts, works, responds to others, whether they are in the right role and what their strengths and weaknesses are).

You may need to spend time explaining the concept of each role and maybe even decide to use a whole lesson on understanding what they are – especially the evaluator's role as this will help the group to see some of their strengths and weaknesses in how they relate to other people.

Once the groups have decided who is going to play each role you can talk them through the remaining four steps.

1. Decide who's doing what.
2. Talk about the challenge and decide on your plan of action.
3. Put the design on paper.
4. Build it.

The task is to build a boat out of newspaper and sellotape that is strong enough to hold a small object while floating in water. The items required for this challenge are plenty of newspaper, one role of sellotape per group, a bowl of water and a small toy. The last two items are for testing the strength of the boats at the end.

The main reason for explaining the above process is to allow the group to discuss as many different options as possible and allow all members to contribute before building actually begins. It also provides time for the designer to use their skills. There should be at least ten minutes of discussion, planning and drawing before they start to construct their boat. Set a time limit for building and off they go.

Discussion and evaluation

Name	
Role played	
What did you like about the role you played?	
What didn't you like about the role you played?	
How did you feel being part of a team?	
Would you play this role again or would you prefer a different one?	
What do you think your strengths are?	
What do you think your weaknesses are?	
How do your answers here compare with the evaluators report?	

Once the time set for the challenge is over and you have tested them all out to see if they is successful, you can choose the option of using the self evaluation form, which are on page 26 of the workbook, or you can hold a whole-group discussion as to how they felt they did individually.

If using the form, you will see that it allows the group to question and describe their own feelings as to how they coped with their role and how they thought they acted as part of the team. It also allows them space to consider what they think are their strengths and weaknesses and what they would change if they did the exercise again.

You should then allow the evaluator to discuss their findings with their group, enabling each person to compare their own thoughts and perceptions of how they performed in a group with the evaluator's report. When working with the evaluator you will need to make sure it is somebody who is fairly articulate and observant and that they know how to offer constructive criticism rather than being negative and even hurtful.

When the task is completed, fill out the evaluation form at the back of this book.

Bringing it all together

The following three statements show the similarities between effective teamwork and friendships. The first is an example of sports teams needing each individual to fulfill their role to obtain success. The second statement highlights the same need for each person involved in a relationship to work with their friends and not against them, to support them through the difficult times in life and help them to develop to reach their full potential. The final paragraph is more directive and gives examples of each other's differences and what our friends can offer the relationship. It also refers to effective friendships being something special that enables us to be ourselves without the need to wear our 'masks' in order to be accepted. The closing comment considers how different our friendships would be if they were like strong and effective teams.

Teams depend on each individual doing their part. A football team will lose if the goalkeeper can't be bothered. They also wouldn't win if the striker didn't want to shoot. Every person in a team has to do their bit to the best of their ability for the team to work and succeed.

It's the same with friendships. If only one friend is willing to make the effort to make it work, the friendship will struggle. Together we can learn and grow from each other's strengths and help each other to develop and accept our weaknesses

In any friendship each person has a role to play. We need to allow our friends to contribute to discussions without laughing at them or blazing them. We need to accept the different roles we play, not everyone will want to do the same as us and vice versa. As a friend we need to have the confidence to play the part we have been created to play, not to have to put on a mask and be someone we are not or don't want to be. Think about your friends, and yourself, and see how different it would be if our friendships were like strong and successful teams.

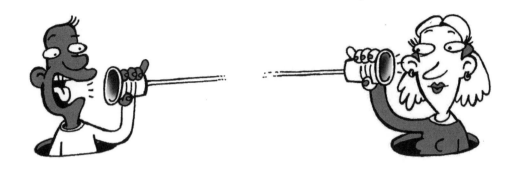

Session 10

The Art of Communication

Session aims

- To help the group to understand the nature and concept of effective communication.

- To help the group to consider the differences between listening and active listening and the need to take time to listen.

- To consider the use of questions for gaining the correct information.

Session background

This final session focuses on the students' need for actively listening to others in such a way that the other person feels valued and truly heard. Everything that we have previously worked on regarding the development of strong friendships would be useless if people didn't take the time to listen.

As the title for this session suggests it really does take a lot of skill and practice to successfully communicate with other people. When somebody is talking to us we can become distracted very easily, our body language can express disinterest, or we can be so consumed with our own problems or thoughts that we fail to actually hear and understand what the other person is really trying to say to us.

The art of communication involves actively listening to the person who is trying to express something to you, understanding exactly what it is they are telling you and showing them that you have understood correctly. If any of these elements of communication are neglected a breakdown in the process is inevitable.

Learning how to communicate effectively takes a long time to learn and this session will hopefully open the students' eyes to a new subject that they can enjoy learning. They will discover the basic principles through the various activities that they will undertake but success will only come with practice.

Icebreaker (optional)

As it is the last session ask the group to choose their favourite icebreaker.

Previous session recap

Last session we took a practical approach to teamwork and did the team challenge. It was interesting to see how an effective team should work and how everyone needs to work together. We briefly considered whether the things that make a team work can help a friendship work – support, sharing, nobody being left out and communication.

Session introduction

Start this session by asking the group if they think the team challenge, that was previously done, would have worked if nobody was allowed to talk. Then ask them what forms of communication they could have used to complete the task? Try to get them to think about the process of communication and after a few answers explain this example as a process for two people exchanging information:

- One person has something to say.

- That person chooses from a variety of methods to get their message across.

- Various things interfere with the message (noise; lack of attention).

- The second person hears the message.

- The second person interprets the message to what they think is being communicated.

- Sometimes the second person repeats what they've heard to see if it's accurate.

The following activities will help the group put these principles into practice.

Code of silence

Activity 1

Form the group into a circle and start a Chinese Whisper. This is where you whisper something in the person's ear on your left and they have to pass it on to the next person and so on around the circle until the last person, the person on your right, whispers the sentence to you. The aim is to see if your original words, said to the first person, have stayed the same or have been changed in anyway. After a few goes add a command to the sentence, for example, 'put your finger in your ear' or 'put your hands in your pockets'. Have a look around the room and see if anyone has not just passed on the whisper but also carried out the command as well. You can comment on how people can get so caught up in the activity or in trying to get the phrase right that they have neglected to do what you have asked them!

Activity 2

How do you hear and understand what is being said to you?

The next exercise allows the pupils to consider how well they can listen and put into practice what they have heard. The group need to work in pairs and they should sit with their backs together either on the floor or on chairs. Both of the pupils should have a pencil and a piece of paper and they need to label themselves 'A' and 'B'. 'A' is going to draw a simple object or picture, like a star or house, and as they go through the process of the drawing they are to describe what they are doing to 'B', however 'B' is not allowed to talk or ask questions. When they have finished have them compare drawings to see how similar they are. Let them change positions so that 'B' draws next.

Activity 3

Another example of active listening is for two people to sit opposite each other and to think of a favourite hobby of theirs. When you say 'go' they both have to talk about their hobby, at the same time, for about thirty seconds. Afterwards ask the group if anyone felt as though they were being listened to.

Then let 'A' describe their hobby again but this time 'B' has to show complete and utter disinterest (like yawning, biting nails, turning around or falling asleep). Once again ask the group if anyone felt as though they were being listened to and ask the 'A's how they felt about being ignored. Get them to change places and do this again. Then discuss how somebody who is actively listening should position themselves and respond to somebody who is talking to them, such as having eye contact, not messing with their hands and asking occasional questions.

Finally ask 'A' to describe their hobby again but this time 'B' is to show positive active listening skills (eye contact, good body position or clarifying questions) and at the end of the time, as part of the conversation, they should repeat back to 'A' what they have said, showing that they have listened properly. Afterwards have a brief discussion as to how 'A' felt this time and then ask them to change places.

Activity summary

After this activity has finished say the following (adapt if necessary):

"Friendships rely greatly on effective communication, often through talking to each other. We may be the type of person who always takes control of the conversations, doing all of the talking and none of the listening. This can often produce a domineering friendship and not an equal and fair relationship. There may well be times in your friendships that you have to put other people's needs before your own and this means that you have to stop talking and listen. It could be that one of your friends is upset and needs you to support them through their problem, but you do not allow them time to talk or show them that you really are concerned by the way you listen. This could cause a problem in your friendship and your friend may question how much you value it. Active listening, understanding and talking are all vitally important in developing effective, supporting and long-lasting friendship."

Activity 4

The final activity in this session requires the group to carefully listen to all the information that they are given, to ask questions and to try and solve a mystery. You can begin by reading out the situation regarding Henry and Harry, on page 23 of the handbook. The students are allowed to ask you any question but your reply can only be either 'yes' or 'no'.

The answer of the riddle is that Henry and Harry are goldfish who are swimming around in their bowl, which is on the sideboard. The family cat has knocked the fish bowl off the sideboard in an attempt to eat the fish but the crashing sound of the bowl has scared the cat away. By the time the owners have arrived home the fish are dead. You can be as creative as you want with the rest of the details.

"You walk into a room and see Henry and Harry lying dead on the floor in a puddle of water".

What happened?

Allow an appropriate amount of time for this as it is the last activity and hopefully one that they will enjoy.

Bringing it all together

This summary relates to the session on communication and it is aimed at helping the group to value their friendships through honestly and openly supporting each other throughout the tough times and the good times.

> Communication is about talking, listening and understanding. It's about allowing time for our friends and them allowing time for us. It's about giving each other quality time to say the things that we really need to say and supporting each other in this. It's about being honest and truthful with each other, being available and putting our friends' needs before our own.

On page 85 you will find 'the final word' which summarises the whole friendship course. True, honest friendship is not something that can be bought or treated lightly, it is something special to be valued and guided at all costs. Real friendship can last for life if those involved respect each other and make themselves available and, when necessary, vulnerable. On a personal note, I only wish that somebody had taught me these foundational principles for building friendships when I was young, as then maybe times in my life wouldn't have been so difficult to cope with on my own.

The final Word

The best thing you could ever have is a real friend. Someone who likes you because of who you are, someone who listens, helps, supports and is always there for you. Someone who helps you to see right and wrong and someone who gently challenges you when you need it.

To find someone so true would be to find the pot of gold at the end of the rainbow.

Are you someone that can be a pot of gold to others? I hope you are.

Appendix

Evaluation sheet

Resources list

Photocopiable session posters

Photocopiable workbook

It Takes Two to Tango Evaluation Sheet

Role played	Leader	Designer	Worker
Name			
How did they behave as an individual?			
How did they behave towards the rest of the group?			
What were their strengths in this role?			
What were their weaknesses in this role?			
How did they cope with authority, discipline, mistakes and criticism?			
How did they perform as part of the team?			
How did the team respond towards them?			

Resources List

Any James Bond Film

Billy Elliot (2000) certificate 15

East is East (1999) certificate 15

Forrest Gump (1994) certificate 12

Four Weddings and a Funeral (1993) certificate 15

Friends series 2 episode 9 (1994)

The Full Monty (1998) certificate 15

I'll Be There For You – The Rembrandts

The Mask (1994) certificate PG

Oliver Twist (1948) certificate U

Peter Pan (1953) certificate U

Stand By Me (1986) certificate 15

Trainspotting (1996) certificate 18

Veggie Tales - Big Ideas Production Inc. (1995)

"Are You My Neighbour?" (Episode 3)

The Wizard of Oz (1939) certificate U

Friendship

the beginning

Life

the reality

The making of a friend

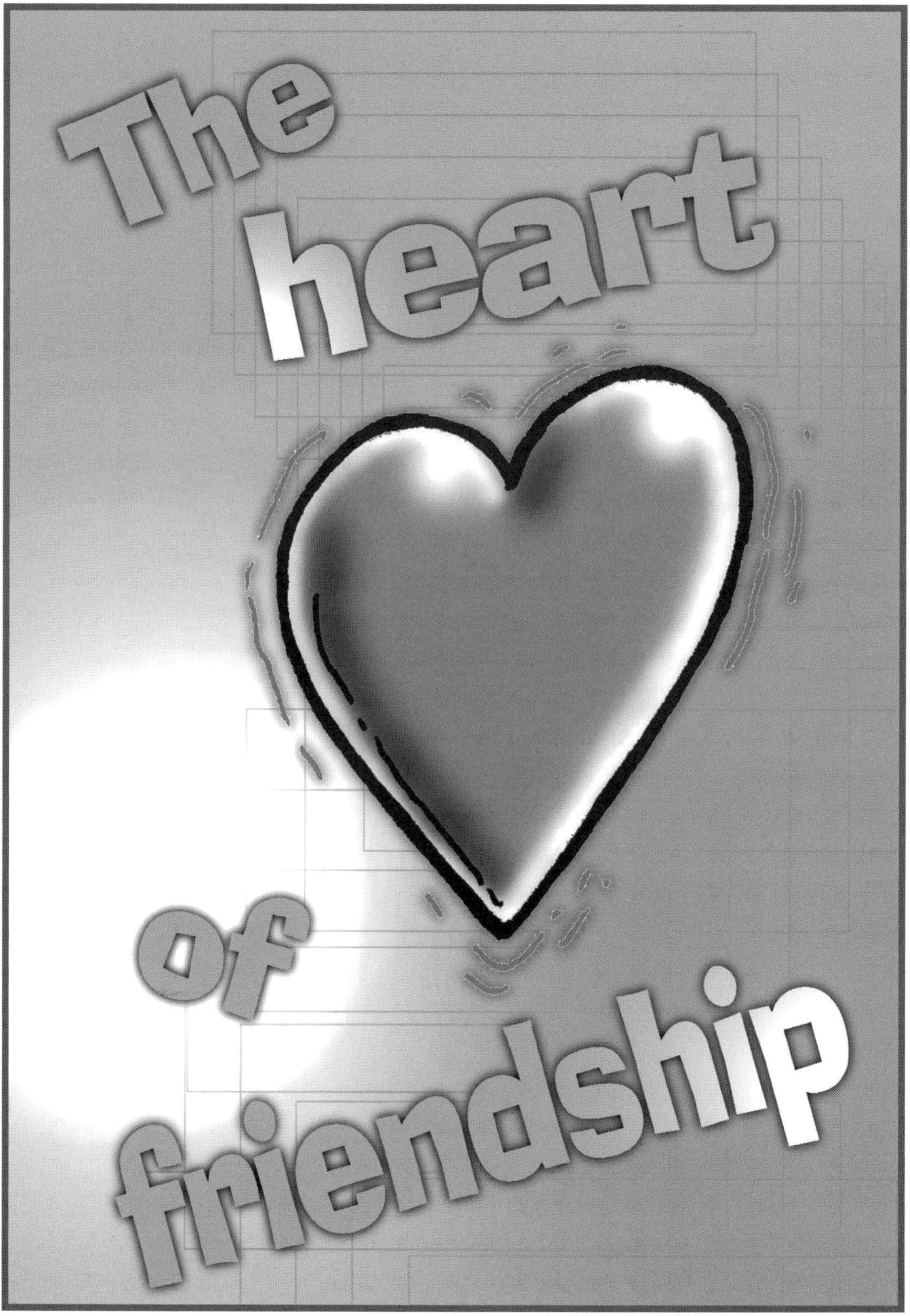
The heart of friendship

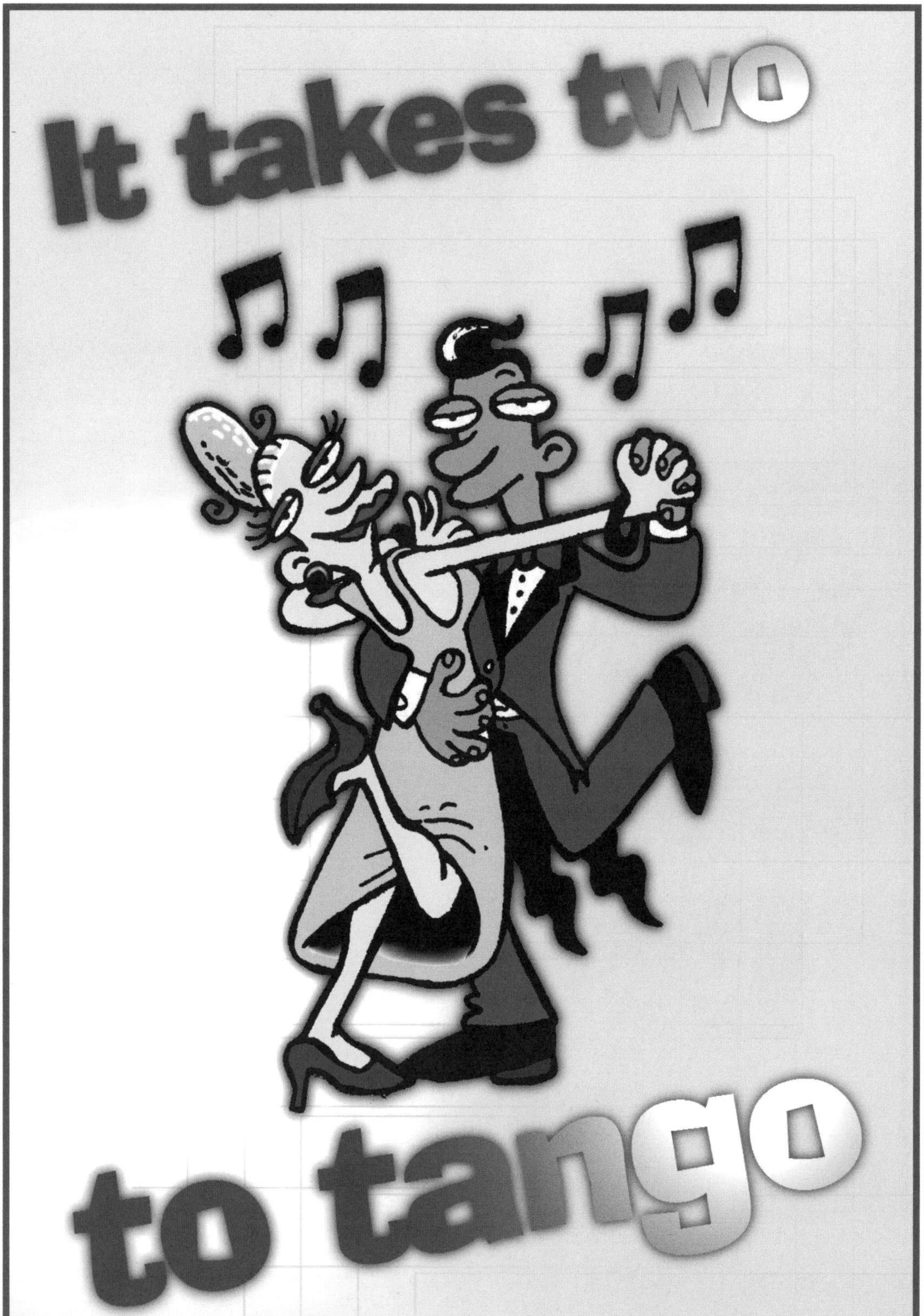
It takes two
to tango

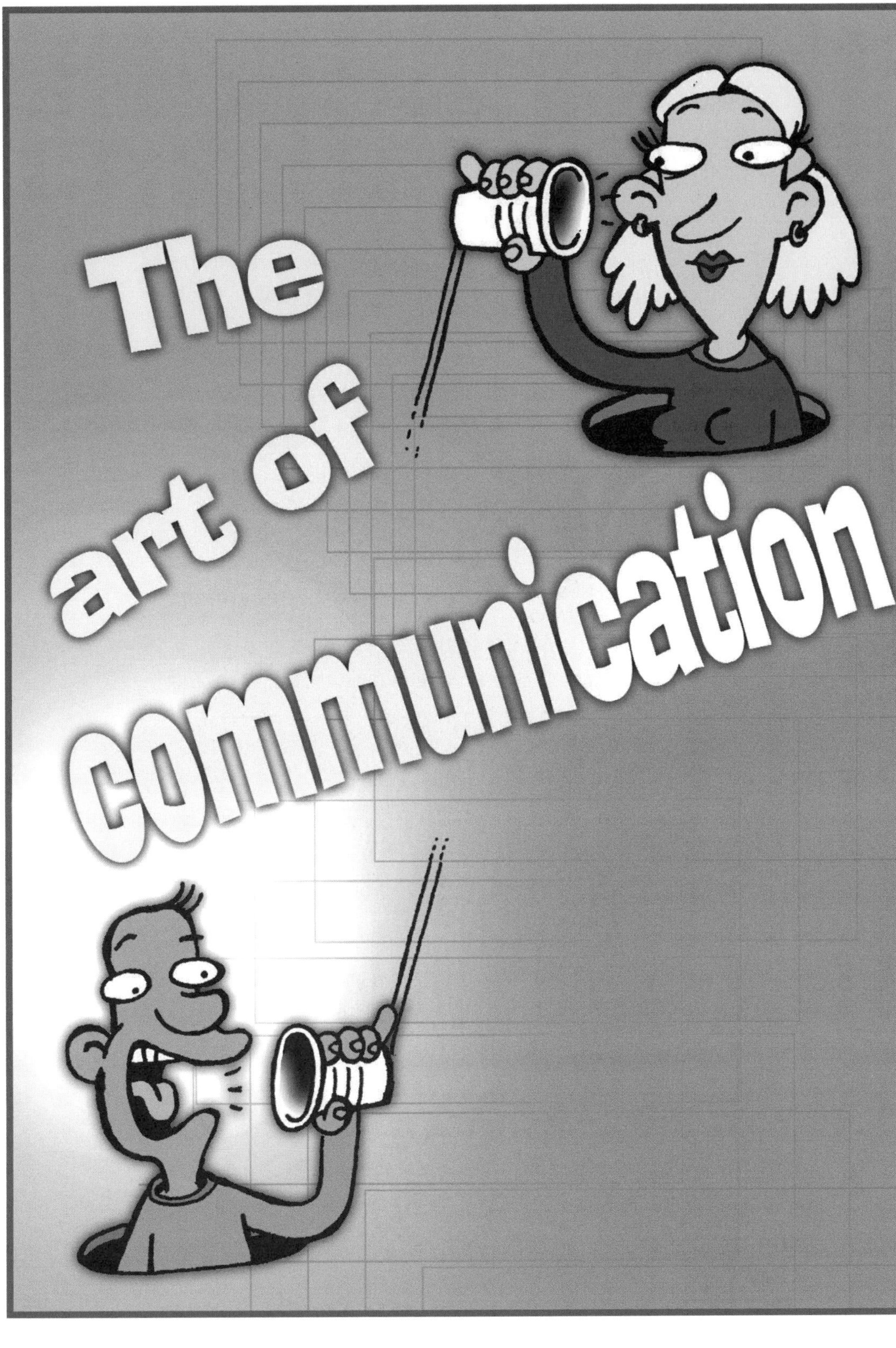
The
art of
communication

Photocopying and Assembling the Student Workbook

The following fourteen pages show the Student Workbook, a set of two workbook pages to each page to make up into an A5, centre stapled booklet.

The pages of the Student Workbook appear to be out of numerical order. This is because we have taken into account how they will appear when you have folded them and assembled the workbook.

To copy and assemble:

1   Set your photocopier to copy at 125% if you are copying to A4 paper.

2   Photocopy the first pages of the workbook as they appear in this book – workbook set of pages 14-15 (opposite).

3   Take this first photocopy and re-feed through your photocopier so that the next set of pages (16-13) can be copied on the reverse.

4   Photocopy set of pages 16-13 onto the reverse of set of pages 14-15. Ensure that these sets are aligned the same way, that is, both sides have the page numbers on the same edge.

5   Repeat this process for all sets of pages. You should have seven double sided sheets of photocopied paper.

6   Ensuring set of pages 14-15 is on the top of the pile and they are all in the same order as they appear in this book, staple the pages along the centre line and fold along this line.

You now have a student workbook.

Instructions for printing the workbook from the CD-ROM are on page 4.

A Unique Individual?

Stanley thought he was a loser. He wanted to be someone else so he put on a mask. Society has not allowed him to be the person he was created to be, Stanley, but to pretend to be someone different.

A healthy self-image gives us confidence.

The Daily Dreamer

How you see yourself is usually different to how other people see you. We look at ourselves and see things we don't like, and then think that other people won't like us because we think we're different.

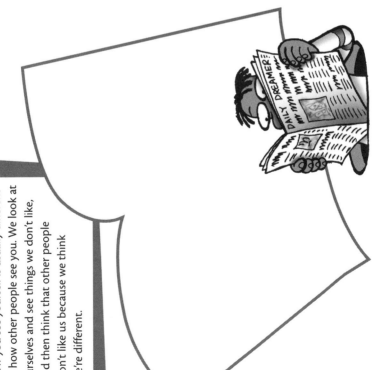

If we want our friends to accept us the way we are, we first need to learn to accept ourselves for who we are.

A Closer Look at Me

My view

My friend's view

A healthy self-image gives us confidence.

valued by others   worthless |⌶⌶⌶⌶⌶⌶⌶⌶⌶⌶⌶⌶| important   not important |⌶⌶⌶⌶⌶⌶⌶⌶⌶⌶⌶⌶|

attractive   ugly |⌶⌶⌶⌶⌶⌶⌶⌶⌶⌶⌶⌶| clever   not very clever |⌶⌶⌶⌶⌶⌶⌶⌶⌶⌶⌶⌶|

loved   not loved |⌶⌶⌶⌶⌶⌶⌶⌶⌶⌶⌶⌶| liked by others   not liked |⌶⌶⌶⌶⌶⌶⌶⌶⌶⌶⌶⌶|

Place an X on the scale lines below at the point that best describes how you are feeling.

Complete this sentence:

I like myself because

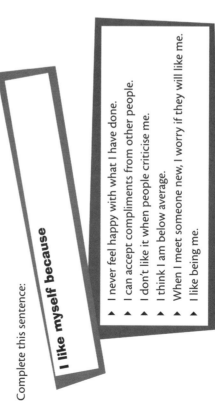

- ▲ I never feel happy with what I have done.
- ▲ I can accept compliments from other people.
- ▲ I don't like it when people criticise me.
- ▲ I think I am below average.
- ▲ When I meet someone new, I worry if they will like me.
- ▲ I like being me.

You are a very special and unique individual. Once you can love yourself because you are you, you can become very good at accepting other people for who they are. This will make you a very, very good friend.

Do I have a choice?

What would make you happy?

What would you change?

The Heart of Friendship

- How would your friends react if they saw you go into a shop and steal some sweets?
- How would your friends react if you tried to get them to do something wrong?
- How would your friends react if you got them into trouble?
- How would your friends react if you were choosing sides in a game and you didn't pick them?

Have your friends got what it takes to be a good friend?

Have you?

The Making of a Friend

Describe the most embarrassing person that you can think of.

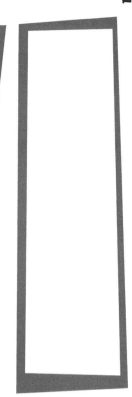

Describe your ideal person.

So, what makes a good friend?

Family

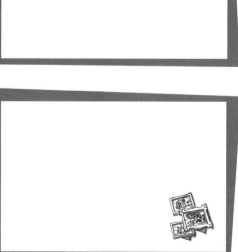

Friends

When you aren't with your friends do you behave differently than when you are with your family?

We all want to be loved and accepted for who we are.

How do you try to be accepted?

How do you think your friends try to be accepted?

It Takes Two to Tango

You are going to attempt a challenge.

Designer

Evaluator

Leader

Worker

Life is a journey.

Some things we can control, some things we can't.

What do we really need to make it through life?

Life – The journey

Is life easy?

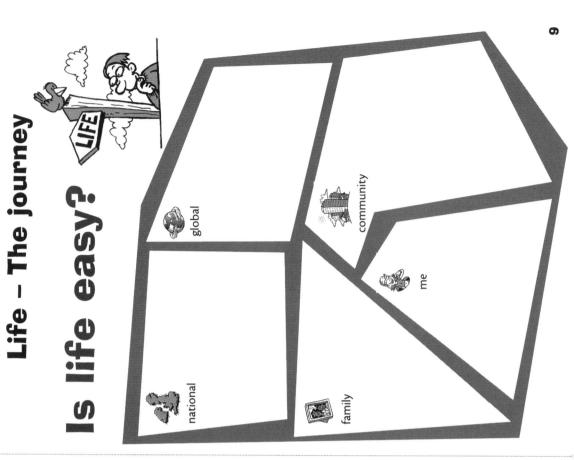

global

national

community

me

family

Steps

1. Decide who's doing what.
2. Talk about the challenge and decide on your plan of action.
3. Put the design on paper.
4. Build it.

When the task is completed, fill out the evaluation forms at the back of this book.

Teams depend on each individual doing their part. A football team will lose if the goalkeeper can't be bothered. They also wouldn't win if the striker didn't want to shoot. Every person in a team has to do their bit to the best of their ability for the team to work and succeed.

It's the same with friendships. If only one friend is willing to make the effort to make it work, the friendship will struggle. Together we can learn and grow from each other's strengths and help each other to develop and accept our weaknesses.

In any friendship each person has a role to play. We need to allow our friends to contribute to discussions without laughing at them or blazing them. We need to accept the different roles we play, not everyone will want to do the same as us and vice versa. As a friend we need to have the confidence to play the part we have been created to play, not to have to put on a mask and be someone we are not or don't want to be. Think about your friends, and yourself, and see how different it would be if our friendships were like strong and successful teams.

Life is hard enough to cope with without other people telling us how we should live, what we should look like and what choices we should make to be accepted.

However, the reality of life is that we need help. We are the only ones who can decide the direction we take – other people can only give us help, options and opportunities.

But – we have to consider, very wisely, the choices we make. Some will be good, some will be bad.

The friends we choose can be good or bad depending on whether they help us grow and support us, or whether they hold us back because they want to make us into something that we don't want to be.

The future is not only a place you are travelling to but a life you are creating.

Friends

Me

The Art of Communication

How do you hear and understand what is being said to you?

If we want friendships to work we have to give each other time to talk and time to listen.

Another way to communicate and make sure you have the right information is to ask the right questions. Here's a game of detectives. You have to solve the puzzle by asking questions.

"You walk into a room and see Henry and Harry lying dead on the floor in a puddle of water".

What happened?

Communication is about talking, listening and understanding. It's about allowing time for our friends and them allowing time for us. It's about giving each other quality time to say the things that we really need to say and supporting each other in this. It's about being honest and truthful with each other, being available and putting our friends' needs before our own.

Life – The Reality

Perceptions of life

Society

Family

Sometimes we find it difficult to get to know people because we are not sure how they will take us. We are all trying to make friends, we want to spend time with people, to talk to them and share stuff with them.

We all need friends and we all need to be a friend!

We need to remember that friends are people and people are potential friends.

The Final Word

The best thing you could ever have is a real friend. Someone who likes you because of who you are, someone who listens, helps, supports and is always there for you. Someone who helps you to see right and wrong and someone who gently challenges you when you need it.

To find a friend so true would be to find the pot of gold at the end of the rainbow.

Are you someone that can be a pot of gold to others?

I hope you are.

Tracy Venables

by Colin McNaughton

Tracy Venables thinks she's great,
Swinging on her garden gate.
She's the girl I love to hate -
'Show-off' Tracy Venables.

She's so fat she makes me sick,
Eating ice-cream, lick, lick, lick.
I know where I'd like to kick
'Stink-pot' Tracy Venables.

Now she's shouting 'cross the street,
What's she want, the dirty cheat?
Would I like some? Oh, how sweet
Of my friend Tracy Venables.

Poem from the book There's an Awful Lot of
Wierdos in our Neighbourhood by Colin
McNaughton.
© 1987 Colin McNaughton
Reproduced by permission of Walker Books Ltd
London SE11 5HJ

Best Friends

by Adrian Henri

It's Susan I talk to not Tracy,
Before that I sat next to Jane;
I used to be best friends with Lynda
But these days I think she's a pain.

I used to go skating with Catherine,
Before that I went there with Ruth;
And Kate's so much better at trampoline:
She's a show off, to tell you the truth.

Natasha's all right in small doses,
I meet Mandy sometimes in town;
I'm jealous of Annabel's pony
And I don't like Nicola's frown.

I think that I'm going off Susan,
she borrowed my comb yesterday;
I think I might sit next to Tracy,
She's my nearly best friend: she's OK.

Reproduced by kind permission of the Adrian Henri estate.

Confusion

1. Untie someone's shoe then tie it up again. Have him sign here:

2. Arm-wrestle someone else and have her sign here when finished:

3. With two other people, sing the first four lines of any nursery rhyme and have them sign here:

4. Find someone with bigger hands than you and have him sign here:

5. Find someone who can say 'hello' in two other languages and have her sign here:

6. Ask someone to draw a picture of their favourite cartoon then sign here:

7. Ask someone to do five press-ups for you and sign here:

8. Ask someone to hop five times on one foot then sign here:

9. Ask five different people to sign his name below:

Team Work Self-evaluation

Name	
Role played	
What did you like about the role you played?	
What didn't you like about the role you played?	
How did you feel being part of a team?	
Would you play this role again or would you prefer a different one?	
What do you think your strengths are?	
What do you think your weaknesses are?	
How do your answers here compare with the evaluators report?	

Friendship – The Beginning

Introduction

This course is aimed at showing you the truth and reality of friendships and whether we should value them and work at them.

embarrassment
fear
isolation

These are feelings that we don't like to experience when we're with other people. We need to try and overcome them.

Time For Fun

Welcome to Friendship

Name

Don't forget to visit our website for all our latest publications, news and reviews.

www.luckyduck.co.uk

New publications every year on our specialist topics:

▸ **Emotional Literacy**

▸ **Self-esteem**

▸ **Bullying**

▸ **Positive Behaviour Management**

▸ **Circle Time**

▸ **Anger Management**

▸ **Asperger's Syndrome**

▸ **Eating Disorders**

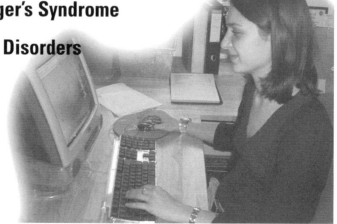